EUTHANASIA

J. SARAVIA

EUTHANASIA
©2025, J. Saravia
ISBN: 978-1-9663370-9-6
Library of Congress Control Number: 2025912614

First Edition, 2025

Printed in the United States of America

Edited by: Sara Khayat
Cover Design by: J. Saravia
Layout Design by: Janis M. Albuquerque

DEDICATION

I dedicate this to relatives, nuclear and chosen family, those who will never know that they have inspired me, and to my past self. Thank you to the Two Spirit and indigiqueer community for uplifting me in ways that have helped me through the process of healing, to families who have invited me into their love and their homes, and to my own family who never gave up on me even in my worst days.

Thank you to the many teachers who have continued to inspire me, who have uplifted me with writing and communal opportunities and recommendations, and who have guided my spiritual, personal and academic journeys. This is but a small list, but thank you to: Mrs. Deborah Fore, my first grade teacher who was the first to ever nourish my writing and my happiness as an abused child, the many science and history teachers who fueled my curiosity and pushed me to move forward, Jon Black and Jeff Odien, who instilled in me a passion for inclusive and memorable pedagogy, Dr. Michael Schwartz, Dr. Larisa Broyles-Chacon, Dra. Valerie Zapata and Professor Ann Pfeifle, who all supported a very misguided youth thirsty to write and be accepted as a queer person. To my instructors at CGU, I thank you also for the continuous patience and training during my graduate years; I am lucky to have received your guidance. To Ceasar and Consuelo, the incredible CLI instructors who provided meaningful feedback and reassurance of the purpose behind my words, this collection would not have been possible without you. To the Season 12 CLI homies: We did it, I thank you, you're all amazing.

To my first teacher, my dear mother Kathy: I cannot express how much
I have learned from you and am grateful for
your continuous whimsy, love and care.
I am honored to be your daughter, above everything else.
You are my entire heart and nothing I do is without you.

To my favorite goddess Mario, former host of the Riverside Underground Performance Organization, and to my fellow performers of the time: I thank you for constantly inspiring me as a poet and a performer, for lending me the first stage to practice and learn what it means to live as a poet. I also want to thank Professor Jo Scott-Coe at Riverside Community College, for further pushing my desire to be on the page by publishing my first poem in "Muse". Thank you also to Sharon Sekhon, who gave me a platform to share my experience in poetry and suicidality for the first time in the 2016 "SHE: Beyond the Paradigms of Pleasure and Peril—A One-day Festival in Honor of Southern California Women."

I also dedicate this collection to those who are experiencing
any form of hardship, loneliness and pain,
as well as those who are gone that have lost the battle.
Know that there is help, and it may take some work, but it can get better.

Acknowledgments

I acknowledge my ancestors, my spirit guides, my friends and family without whom the creation of this work would not be possible. To my grandmothers and the women who have guided me in understanding the necessity for art and the men who have guided me in the development of strength. To those who claim no and/or all gender, may you also be acknowledged within these pages in tenderness.

To my past selves who have lived and died many times over, I acknowledge your existence, your resistance, your resilience, and your fear.

EUTHANASIA

TABLE OF CONTENTS

PART ONE: PRE-FUNERAL

PART TWO: BURIAL

PART THREE: RESURRECTION

AUTHOR'S PLAYLIST

This playlist will go in chronological order, beginning with the song that was playing when I came into this world to the music I am revisiting and have had on during the creation of this anthology. As a child witha parent musician, I was exposed to a lot of different genres and types of music, and would be honored if you took the audible journey with me alongside the words I've provided for you on the page. This is not an extensive playlist of everything I have listened to, but one I felt would be appropriate to work for each section of the book, in the order I recommend.

Fair Warning: Much of this music varies, and includes really loud rock.

Pre-Funeral
The Awakening—Pat Metheney

Mrs. Robinson—Simon & Garfunkel

I Love You Always Forever—Donna Lewis

No Rain—Blind Melon

Love is Like a B utterfly—Dolly Parton

Tren al Sur—Los Prisioneros

Mariposa Traicionera—Maná

Run to You—Whitney Houston

Rocket Man—Elton John

Take Five—Dave Brubeck

Dreams—Fleetwood Mac

Don't Dream It's Over—Crowded House

Losing my Religion—R.E.M.

Duvet—Boa

Hasta Que Te Conoci— Juan Gabriel

Crazy Love—Poco

Sweet and Low—Augustana

Clair De Lune—Claude Debussy

Kiko and the Lavender Moon—Los Lobos

Cough Syrup—Young the Giant
Waiting—Green Day
Es Por Ti—Juanes
On & On—Erykah Badu
Starry, Starry Night—Don McLean

Burial
Paper Flowers—Evanescence
Blue Jeans—Lana Del Rey
Dark Blue—Jack's Mannequin
Satellite—Guster
Atlas—Coldplay
Burn—The Cure
Despre Tine Cant—Dan Balan
Seize the Day—Avenged Sevenfold
Where Eagles Dare—Legacy of Brutality
All Apologies—Nirvana
Til the End—My Chemical Romance
Breaking the Habit—Linkin Park
The Red—Chevelle
Dead Memories In my Heart—Slipknot
No One Knows—Queens of the Stone Age
Got the Life—Korn
Monsoon—Tokio Hotel
Fell on Black Days—Soundgarden
Back to Black—Amy Winehouse
Closer—Kings of Leon
Russian Roulette—Rihanna
Love Hurts—Incubus
Don't Speak—No Doubt
Cry Like a Rainstorm—Linda Ronstadt
What the Water Gave Me—Florence and the Machine
Dancing with a Stranger—Sam Smith, Normani
Running Up that Hill—Kate Bush
Diamonds and Rust—Joan Boaz

Hurt—Johnny Cash
Midnight—Coldplay
Reckoner—Radiohead
Boyfriends—Harry Styles
Varúð—Sigur Rós
Tenderly—Chet Baker

Resurrection
Overthrown—Pinegrove
Délivrance—Alcest
Magic—Coldplay
Goodbye Yellow Brick Road—Elton John
Last Train Home—Pat Metheney
Cumbia de los Muertos—Ozomatli
Sisters—Halluci Nation
Bleed Well—H.I.M.
Zero—Smashing Pumpkins
Good Morning Heartache—Billie Holiday
Lobo-Hombre en Paris—Mil Siluetas
No Me Conoces—Marc Anthony
Pure—Matte Blvck
Wildflower—Billie Eilish
Por Una Mujer Bonita—Pepe Aguilar
Everlong—Foo Fighters
All I Wanted- Paramore
Like a Stone—Audioslave
Fire and Rain—James Taylor
Hay Unos Ojos—Linda Ronstadt
Lover, Please Stay—Nothing but Thieves
Chasing Pavements—Adele
Messy—Lola Young
Long, Long Time—Linda Rondstadt
Dust in the Wind—Kansas
The Ghost of You—My Chemical Romance

These Dreams—Heart

Hasta La Raiz—Natalia Lafourcade

Where Have all the Cowboys Gone?—Paula Cole

In My Place—Coldplay

Come Undone—Duran Duran

Angel from Montgomery—Bonnie Raitt

Constant Craving—K.D. Lang

A Lot—21 Savage

Je te Lasserai des Mots—Patrick Watson

The Night We Met—Lord Huron

What Once Was—Hers

Light my Love—Greta Van Fleet

Year of the Cat—Al Stewart

I'm Still Standing—Elton John

EUTHANASIA
—THE EXPLANATION—

Euthanasia: A response and exploration in three chapters of the darkest moments of my life, including but not limited to: death/dying, relations to the body, death of the self, medicine/hospitals, needles, the color black, the idea of blood, physical and mental distress, trying but not being able to participate in screaming, long hallways.

This collection also serves as an artistic mechanism to explore healing, why I was so angry as a traumatized child, youthful and intensive instances of all kinds of abuse, loss and betrayal and at the end, soothing myself while also remembering.

—THE STRUCTURE—

Chapter 1: Pre-Funeral

This section will focus on my life before the complete descent of my mental state. Before I began abusing myself after years of others abusing me, and not understanding how to cope with that. The early times of being small, and finding small joys within me when I was facing colossal pain, a state that I have found myself going back to at the end.

Chapter 2: Burial

The deep dive into the darkest moments of my life. Riddled with coming face to face with my trauma, realizing all of those things that had and at the point continued to happen to me, and feeling like I had no way out. An independent encounter with emotional instability, substance abuse and multiple rounds of insanity.

Chapter 3: Resurrection

The bounce back into myself and into real life. Deep moments of recovery and reflection, though by no means completely void of having to confront my past and work through what I now know to be generational trauma and curses, life long journeys in recognizing myself as someone with an addictive personality and who deserves all the happiness I was denied in my younger years.

Trigger Warnings:

Death, Dying, Incest, Rape, Abuse, Self-Harm, Substance Abuse, Mental Health, Suicide, Abandonment, Body Image, Domestic Violence, Genocide, Euthanasia
Please read with caution and at your own pace.

Dear Reader,

However you choose to approach reading this collection, I wish you to go on this journey with me carefully and in your own time. Please pace yourself, remember to breathe, and if at any point you feel over-whelmed with what I have to share with you, do not hesitate to pause.

As this volume deals with the relationship between art and death and dying, please lean heavily on your own intuition, on the communities and loved ones around you, and the resources that I have provided at the end of this book.

Be well.

PART ONE: PRE-FUNERAL

THE BUILDING WITH THE ORANGE BLOSSOMS OUT FRONT

I went down that old same road with my mother a few days ago,
though it was funny to think that she was in the passenger seat. I've
only recently told her that I was happy she did—I am forever grateful
to my mother for that.

It's an old building in an old town with old orange trees in front of it:
the most soothing thing I remembered, going in. I was scared as hell
going in, which I'm sure translated to everyone in the waiting room.
I tried to look so tough. I sat there silently, like everybody else, but
I could hear the waves of tears inside me; gathering up in delicate
drops that bounced off the walls of my heart like raindrops on glass.
I could hear everything, but said nothing.

Until I got into my psychiatrists' room.

She was warm, kind & elderly—exactly the kind of person who—
(I wouldn't admit it then)—I wanted to be like when I grew up. She
sat in front of me and I remember the low light that made me feel safe,
like I didn't need permission to settle in. In this space, I could be cozy
and all the secrets scattered in all corners of the room could eventually
come out of hiding. And they did.

She went down the list of disorders, feelings, howisitwhenyouarehome
that I'm sure she knew some of due to the frantic nature of my mother.
Aside from the blossoms, it was the way she first caught me that sticks
out in my mind. This interaction was slow and quick, but even now
still seems unreal. I listened to myself answer 'yes' or 'no', where in
my final answer, she caught me on a wire.

It was just one question:
"Cutting or self harm?"

I answered no, but tugged on my left sleeve, begging in my mind that
she did not see.
She did.

TWO HANDS

I remember as she died, my aunt recalled a dream where god held them in two hands. She and my grandmother were cradled in each and eventually, she was let go; but my grandmother was taken. Not too long after, she died.

She died around 4 in the morning, and I remember sleeping next to my brother because neither of us wanted to be alone; I woke up a few minutes after the report says she took her last breath. When my parents came in to tell us that she was gone a few hours later, I told them I already knew.

Now when I sit here between my other abuela and my mom, I reach out to hold each of their hands. I have held each of their hands separately in the hospital, each looking up at me, trying not to cry, knowing full well we all needed to. We have all had a hard time with that, but because of the state of their hearts, we have all allowed ourselves to do so.

These hands that were once young, now stretched by the widths of time; over hot stoves, under budding children. Polished sometimes, at different times of the year, different colors. The rough hands from years of immigrant work, holding hands of others' children and scrubbing floors of their homes. Hands that sweat from not being able to pay the A/C bill during a California summer, hands that never shook under the pressures of the ER, hands that grow pain from years in sweatshops that turn dresses by the dollar into fashion that cost fortunes.

Tissues in hand, hands in hands, pulses displayed on monitors from devices connected to fingers. We wet our fingers with the tears that fall on the back of these hands. I have never wiped back their tears before, felt the weight of the beginning of a cleanse.

Then comes the change.

They will both need to keep up with regular testing, constant phone calls, plenty of rounds of hospital visits; for now, I hold both hands as I sit between them. Their pulse is mine, *sangre* in me, *cuerpos* reinvented in three generations; but in the aftermath, I see the complications of my grandmothers' hands.

These hands that hold have once held me, and I laugh and sing,
    like when I was a little girl.
These hands that hold a book of poetry to soothe the wounds
    inflicted by her sons.

These hands that hold her children from being beaten,
    which I'd mimic with my siblings.
These hands that are learning to hold on again,
    that I never want to let go.

These hands that hold all things, hold my heart; hold my life.
These hands that also let me go, struck my mother, let bitterness win.

How many times I have   Learned to love you   And then
                             Let you go

ALLEYWAYS

Mijas lost to dark alleyways
I think of these words
From another book
I think of who I was in a past life
Spread out, lost and then found
Who would it have been
To have found me?

What kind of spirit would I be?
I think where I would have to return to
Those houses, those memories
Maybe it would be easier for me
To return back to places
And not back to anyone

My body gently scraped off the ground
Or perhaps, that is the feminine imagination
I'm being taken care of better
In death than in life
I think this death would not hit anyone
Too hard

Cradled to the hard table, between slabs of gray
Who would come to take me?
My energy, my spirit, taken somewhere else
I hope in every round of reincarnation she is happy
That gentleness need not wait until the grave
And that I am not found in too many alleyways

PRE-FUNERAL

Why can't everybody understand
That suicide
Is like a pre-funeral

When you get to see
Who actually cares about you
An elated feeling

A sigh of relief
At the prospect of the end
Misery shatters

When the same energy is felt
When everybody says,
"Aw, it's too bad we
     Have to get together this way"

What if instead of answering the call
That tells you not to be here
You get a call
From someone
Who was just asking for help

QUASI-IMPULSIVE

I go back, in and out
Out and around and back again
It finds me, then runs
Over and over again

"Suicide acts as quasi-impulsive"

Stops by sometimes, and holds me tight
Its visits in these moments feel never ending
Quasi—as in sometimes
And sometimes, almost, I want to give in

Ideation

        To

                Action

Action

        To

                Extinction

Not this time, I try to be fine, tears fall, once again
Pulse to impulsive
Well considered acts because I am not well
Lethality methods   slow   me   down
Strong death wish enclaves evolve into full flesh, end of flesh,
suicidal processes
Treatments try to emerge
But I do not know how I will find myself
Know that these thoughts will still be quasi-impulsive
But I feel my pulse—tell me how to be alive

Extinction
            To
                        Action

Action
            To
                        Ideation

EUTHANASIA, DIAGNOSIS I

I grow more concerned for myself
Studying what I am as I stand before the glass
Becoming someone . . . Something . . . Else
Paintings on the walls watch over me
But the house overtakes me
And suddenly
I
  Am
     Surrounded
By thin walls of familiar pain
Bruises in my brain of what I didn't want to be true
Unraveling shrouds, unnatural thoughts
Everything comes rushing in at once
Everyone becomes an unfamiliar figure
And the worst curse of all wakes up within me:

                        I remember.

ALEXITHYMIA

As in the inability to know about one's own emotions
The inability to feel comfortable with the self
In watching the self-deteriorate and die
                    And decay
                    And die

In getting too anxious when they don't respond
As in knowing it's not their fault for what others did to you
The inability to feel comfortable with the feelings
And you can't trust the lies that bend into truths

            Where you just want to be normal
            Where you just want to be fine
            Where you just want to be yourself

AGONY

Have you ever heard the agony of a woman
The sounds of her sinking her teeth
Into her own flesh
To keep from learning about how to express herself
Apologizing for every hour of her existence
And begging for kindness, when darkness craves more
Bore witness to the hell of owning a body
That brings life even when the one she loves
May not want her alive at all
Breaking her own bones to stir the family meal
Give away the hands that were meant to feel silk
Pour out her soul so that others may drink
Have you ever wondered what happens
When she gives everything
And has finally had enough

DARKNESS

I wonder what
My ancestors felt
When they looked
Into the darkness

What did
The threat of
Emptiness
Mean to them?

How they might
Have celebrated
A different kind
Of death

Approaching the trees
Forests with warped branches
With a lunar accompaniment
What was on their mind?

THE BABE'S LAMENT

Unjustify my euthanasia, because I am done
Over the chronicles and volumes of pain
Feeling that I am old and that my life has just begun
You can argue about the state of my
Dead, unbeating heart tomorrow
Fight with the lawyers, coroners turned criminals
For me, it will not matter
        Your decisions, I will not hear
May the medics require that you brush my hair
Sing me a lullaby, remind me that I am loved
Take their time to put the babe to sleep
One last time
Anonymous death dweller:
        Am I just a patient to you?
        What do you think of me
        That I've reached you so soon?
Justify my death as you see fit
Write down my demise in piles of papers
        Fit the clothes laid for me before you
        Will her to a final goodbye, eternal sleep

                                        Let them fight outside
                                        I am not here anymore

TOMORROW

Where you will be:
　　Who or what you'll transition to
I wish you could be where I am today
Now, more than ever, I am so scared for tomorrow
Don't want to keep asking who I might lose next
And for many that I do
　　It won't be their fault
They do not want to leave me either, go to glory so soon

Don't want to lose me either

How can I help them here, keep them from floating away
I want them here forever
　　Tomorrow and today
Rock them into quiet nothing so they have no fear
So that I do not feel fear for them also
Hear no news, pass no laws, have no worries
That make them wish
　　For something better

I don't want to fear
That to my loved ones
I won't be able to say

I'll see you tomorrow

PART TWO: BURIAL

SILLY GIRL, SPILLING GHOSTS

they come out of you
	everywhere you go
ghouls and ghosts
	become your friends
hold your hands
	cover your eyes
push needles into veins
	liquid gold, blackened body
haunting you is too easy
	ghosts and ghouls
love you
	dance when you die
come alive
	when you cry
silly girl, spilling ghosts
	you are not a woman
death is enticing
	take it in your hands
the hands that
	the ghouls hold
march forward
	do not go back
no more goodbyes
	push the needle harder
it will not pain you
	you will be over soon

LIMBS

When the limbs don't do
as they are told
there is an unfolding in the ether
telling them the past is no longer available

the body does not move
the body does not move
the body cannot move

When the arms
can no longer hold
and the hands cannot hold another
it is hard to find worth in life

the body does not move
the body does not move
the body cannot move

When the legs
don't know how to hold up
and the feet can't go forward
all feels lost

the body does not move
the body does not move
the body cannot move

It is the brain that does it the worst
bullies and commands
but the commands do not go
and the limbs are futile

the body does not move
the body does not move
the body cannot move

ADDICTION'S ANONYMOUS

Oh, how deliciously tempting am i
    i am your favorite
    i come in all forms, and i am hard to avoid
You may try, but i peak out every now and again
        and you know it
            and you love it
i am a fun time when you let me
i am grasping your throat when you do not
    grasping
Like a tiny hand, i hold you deep to cage your voice
i come in many forms: drugs, guns, blades, ropes
      all kinds
and i have many names: but you are still naming me
i am open
        in your heart, i hold a hefty weight
A dark balance that you try to run away from
    you need me
It's a little like how i appeared, as apple to eve
But you haven't built you own garden
She had the task of putting a label on everything
So what will you name me, broken Eve?
    temptation, addiction, recovery, sobriety, relapse
    temptation, addiction, discovery, rehab, repeat

i am the cracks on the sidewalks you step on
  The bright light from the sun that glows beneath your eyes
  The shooting stars that take a trip around the moon
i am joy that you find when you try to leave
  The laughter of children, those who are strangers and eventually
  your own
    The poems that you write, i guide the pen
There is no need for formalities between us
  you know who i am and i—i know you
  i've been there, when you've inhaled and smothered your lungs
  pierced your skin when you didn't know how to be quiet
  around your neck: in the garage, your room, the bathroom
While no one is watching
    but i was there
There is no way for you to get lost in paradise
  god will not save you and neither will i

i don't expect that you'll always know how to save yourself

    but i'd like to see you try.

HAUNTED HOUSE

In the summer, I brush up against the trees
   Looking for solace and shade
Away from the sun, my foundation is wet
   How I groan in the winter
My bones feel pain and I am alone
   Even the trees cannot comfort me
For they are bare
   On their own, dying
Dark shadows run inside me
   Ghosts crawl across my floor
People hate me
   They say the wrong things
Misinterpret my visage
   Getting more scared with each night
But I shine brightly under the moon
   And to the right people, I am inviting
We spend lots of time together
   I often hold in their conversations
Within my walls are words no one else will hear
   No one else will understand
Yet I hold on to them anyway
   At times I have visible windows

See through and transparent
      When close enough, I may
Let you see through me
      The old crown molding, once new
In some places torn to shreds
      By unworthy hands
Yet I abstain an old charm
      Sometimes beauty
The winds and the thieves have not
      Totally destroyed me
I still stand, even under others' threats
      Not understanding me
      When they look at me
There is no value that they see
      But in a time gone past
Old enough for me to turn away from
      I once was a pile of bricks under the rain

I am a haunted house that no one wants to write about
But someday—
      Someday—
            They will

PAST.

the girl from the asylum
visits me every so often
gets nestled in my head
and reminds me
that we were already here
around, i circle
the lake
lamps reflect into
dark waters
where i walked with
the doctor
he spares me pain
Herr Doktor
though i have to
go back to it
the chambers
echo
i get called from
halls below
the catacombs
are open again
and i return to them
diseased angel
living amongst the spirits

BKTS RESPONSE

"The complexities of traumatic memory"
Is hard for me to read
Because it is an endless web
Of a mess I did not ask
To be tangled in
Caught up in things
I should not have been
Asked to be a certain way
I should not have been
You asked so much of me
A lot of really big things
When I was so little
I have to soothe her now
Because you won't
You never did
You never have

Panic attacks—seizures—"epileptic fits"

What do you do when you are traumatized by a bed?

GLOOM

Gloom weighs heavy on me
I see it outside
Outside– as the rain falls
A mix of gray clouds and green trees

My fever burns in the rain
Drops of water melt into me
My skin, alight with this sickness
I cannot escape

But then I feel the rain again
And I am cold
My body changes so quickly
And I remember I can adapt

Not an overstayed welcome
My temperature changes
And I think of the old ways
Of listening to the rain

Why do people ask
The rain to go away?
I always want it
To stay

IN/OUT PAIN

Inflicting pain
Seemed so easy for you
"You lie"
"Not true"
"You exaggerate"

You say

I wish
I wish I could say I could
I wish I could say
I could
Say
That these things never happened to me

How can I doubt myself?
My brain/ my body
We remember

I just get so tired of you
Squeezing what's in my mind
Twisting
Doubting
Thinking I am lying

I wish
I wish I was
Why would you wish I wasn't?

EYES + PTSD

Again
The concept of eyes
Comes back again

The eyes inform the trauma
The trauma informs the eyes

I sometimes cannot see
The pain before me

Anticipate
It fading
Going away

But is burned within me
Even if it is pain
I cannot see

BLACK-BLACK-BLACK

black-black-black
I am devoid of feeling
I am not sad nor ashamed
the season of dead will come

and i embrace it
gladly
i miss those old buildings and headstones
i miss going to another time

i twist expectations
and death twists with me
is it possible to be happy
and love death?

ANOTHER PTSD CASE

*"The most striking difference between normal controls and
survivors of chronic trauma was in activation of the prefrontal
cortex in response to a direct eye gaze. The prefrontal cortex
(PFC) normally helps us to assess the person coming toward
us, and our mirror neurons help to pick up his intentions.
However, the subjects with PTSD did not activate any part
of their frontal lobe, which means they could not muster any
curiosity about the stranger."*

I hate reading about myself medically
It means
That I must confront the truth

EYES that see in black and white
What others think of me
Pain in print

EYES that are meant to imagine
And not meant to realize
The brain is broken

EYES that cannot always see
Because of
What You Did To Me

EYES that read the medical reports
Can't visualize the danger
Coming straight to me

EYES too fearful of the gaze
Lest we become aware of
What Has Happened To Me

PURPLE FINGERS OF PROMETHEUS

I remember the face
My mother made when she saw
The purple finger marks around my throat
She and I listening
To a reading of Frankenstein years later
I wondered as the creature took the lives
Of three victims—how easily that could have been me
My own creature's rage, rich with insecurity
The mortician, looking down upon me
        How they'd pity me.
I remember looking at myself in the mirror
The red flush face that would for a while
Turn back to meet
My attempted assassin
Like Justine: underwent trials, blamed myself
For a time, accepted that this would be my life
And my death
The blow to my jaw,
The same jaw on the same mouth you expected to give you an apology,
That now speaks of your kind of monstrous frustration
That I know that I did not deserve to die from
You never again will wrap your hands around my throat
Or see the face of my mother who also escaped her creature
Both of us lucky to have escaped: lucky to still be alive
Burying bones of the past that haunt our bodies
The pain is still alive
Burning letters where only once you proclaimed your love
At least the creature was honest
Confessed to his crimes, a wandering sinner
Your demands as a mate were too much for me
And so
My creature
You will forever roam alone

THREE SUICIDES

With every death comes a sacrifice
While I find myself
Continuing to find meaning
Those that give me that chance
Are far deeper
      Into the ground

I don't always know them all
      There's been
      Mention
      And application
Of three suicides lately
 and they all get
 under my skin

So I lean in
      under the sun
      and the apricot tree
      green fruit surrounds me
      and i feel them

They tell me to cry
      and hold tight to the grass
      so i weep
      I feel them strongly
      they tell me to let go
      and the grass
      turns into hands

I feel dark forces
    leaving me
    giving into the wind
    and hiding in every corner
    but I don't feel them
    lurking anymore

But I do feel the breeze
    it welcomes me back
    brings me back to life
    and i am surrounded
    by a thick wall
    of sadness and gratitude

I believe in their sacrifices
I believe in using the powers
That they stored
For their own life
To protect – use in my own

Death may be a frequent visitor
I don't think I'll
Fully get used to it
But I have to remember
Their sacrifice

HOW DO YOU SURVIVE

When the people around
You don't

How do you survive
Knowing that they didn't want to
So you put on a brave face
In unspoken words
Knowing everything is not fine

I have survivor's guilt
Every time, when
The ones around me
Don't want to be here anymore

How can I convince them
That it's worth it
When I don't
Even know myself

MISSING

I almost lost him again
He was found eventually
Thank god

But I almost lost him again

I'll probably never know why
Why he chose to go for the gun
The same gun that could have been shot
The same gun that could have killed him

How could that be any better
Than falling from the eighth floor

So now he is watched
We, too, are watching him
In a little room with plastic chairs
We ask, "How are you?"
Ignoring the situation, but it lingers in the air

It is a tragedy
That people can live
Under the same roof
And want to die in different ways

He just got caught

He calls me
Early in the morning—apologizing
"Apologizing for what?", I say
Every morning I am greeted with:
    "Hey Jess, it's me"
My daily blessing to hear

FLOWERS IN THE GRAVE

I wonder if I'll be able to smell the flowers you put on my grave
I imagine that if I wiggle inside
You'll see me
Working, clawing, making my way to you
Would you put flowers on me if you saw me then?
I would worry you, scare you, I wouldn't be myself
Monstrous and vague; no resemblance to the person I once was
I shutter at the thought of Catholic beads and caffeinated hallelujahs
And ask for a mountain of flowers instead
I ask my death not be in vain, rather that I am covered in plants' veins
Because those feel more valuable to me
If my lover lasts longer than I, may they lay alongside me
Adorn the tomb I sleep in with imminent fragrance
Sleep with me above, while I struggle down below
Before they close the casket
Before they say goodbye
Place orange blossoms in my hair
Roses on my temples, wisteria on my wrists
Blossoms all over, as you place me under
I ask in lieu of sorrow
That there be flowers in the grave

ROSES

I desire roses
After many fields
Of dead tulips

Old flowers
Dried in the sun
And not for me

In all colors
A range of fragrances
That's my desire

Good riddance
To prickly thorns
Piercing my fingertips

Throw petals in the wind
Have them caress my face
And kiss the weeds away

DESOLATE ROSES

Desolate roses in the street
Feel the Earth beneath concrete
And down beneath the Earth and concrete
Are bodies that we'll never meet
Roses bloom in bushes from dead
Morsels that smell sweet overhead
Sun rays blossom and vapors purge
When bodies move and flowers emerge
Desolate roses in the street
Feel the Earth beneath concrete
With vines cupped in pricks
And petals thick with growing twists
Of every color and every size
The bodies below do prophesize
Of bones at brittle brink
Minds grow cold and brains don't think
And death of old age
Make dead ones come out from their rage
Hands of women, held babies past
My do these babies grow so fast
Death comes in and acts so sly
And then back to sleep do these old ones lie
Arrangements are made, funerals all neat
Crying comes and goes, emotion cycles complete

    And after the procession
    The mummies
    Awaken

The tombstones here over time grow abandoned,
    old embellishments now command them

Desolate roses in the street
Feel the Earth beneath concrete

BEND

The flowers bloom and so do I wither
Remnants of memories grasp what the sun used to do for me
But I cannot weep
Leaves, tender
Stems on the bend
I grow old and the more I bend, bend, bend
Old tombs and concrete crypts greet me
And my spirit lingers in the wind by the trees
Watching, where I will sleep, this place will do
Nicely, I see how many other people
Will bend

To see me one more time
Remember the girl from the hood
Making unluck literary
Dug myself from my misfortune
Words on ghetto stones
Crossed out of history
But down on the concrete
A pollution of crosses
Back to the barrio
These spray painted streets will always be home

I will not feel the tears that fall on my open face
My death blossoms, and so do I celebrate
How much others celebrate me
But then comes the time when I must leave
And look to collections of flowers left for me
Splashing bouquets of a million goodbyes
Voices walk away from where I rest
Only the trees above me will remain
And I hope that through me
New flowers will emerge

EUTHANASIA, DIAGNOSIS II

There is a strange sound of a knife
That I hear echo from upstairs
Screams soak into the walls at home
And I find myself wondering
If I will make it through the night

Down the street, my friends are sleeping
Unaware of the madhouse I live in
Where knives are pulled out of drawers
Glistening with threat to cut under the skin

Cartoons get the sound of knives right
The silly shing is something tragic for me now
These weapons escape their temporary prison
And charm with big teeth: temptations of violence

My mother on this night finds herself
Near the end of the blade in my father's hand
And she's frightened in a way that I have never heard
Before

At 13, I think of the small decision to sacrifice myself
Get shredded up to keep her and my siblings safe
I think, *ohgod*, I blink and wonder what to do
Whether to make a call, whether to make a noise, whether to run

All the choices make me feel that
At the end of the night I will taste my own blood
The blade will be used not towards my grown mother
Or siblings, but on my childish body

And then, when I have finished all this thinking,
I hear the knife return back to the drawer
I fly to each room, and see my brother and sister, asleep and still safe
Confirming that my sacrifice would have been worth it
It would be years later that my diagnosis
A jumbled cocktail of acronyms
Would emerge from that night, when I would start
Forming marks on my arms, voluntary blade to skin

Jailed in the bathroom, my blood would run
And I remembered the sound of that knife
Binding myself night after night
To that memory

I would have let him kill me for you. I wonder how Mom would have
felt, seeing me split so freely after so many years of seeing other
people's blood in the trauma centers where she worked. How would
she feel, knowing she could not save me, but could save everybody
else. Other people. Other children. Other people's children.

I would have been another dead patient who might have had
something to live for.
"Died at the hands of her father," disguised as child fatality on the
coroner's report. What else would that paper say—would the coroner
shake his head?

Would my father have carried the cremations of the
Corpse that he created? Would he go on living?
His acts of cowardice tell me that yes—he would

But when I think of the decision that he almost made me have to make
I would die all over again

KARMA KEEPS THE SCORE

It's interesting
  Who people choose
To hang out with
  Very interesting
I see the photos
  Of different bodies
Behind the camera
  But they all
Make me feel the same
  Exes, family, friends
Smiling, eating, chatting
  My ghost is in
Every photo
  I press my presence
Against my phone's glass
  My fingers 'x' out
Of their image
  I hope that they
Do not bother me

  But my quick heartbeat
Tells me: do not lie
  I see every problem
From these problem people
  Rise again
Behind their eyes
  My eyes
Grow red
  And I am angry
Angry that they
  Experience joy
Imitative bliss
  While I
Do not forget
  Surely they don't either

But their happiness
      Makes my pain
Feel invisible
      When I hear
My mother weeping
      As she cries,
            "But they know
                  What he has
                        Done to me"
They know
      And it is in
That knowing
      That the pain
Continues to grow
      There is so much
We could do
      I want to run
I want to shout out
      To all those
Motherfuckers
      Who spent time
Hurting
      My mother

Who used energy
      To hurt me
I want to climb
      To Mount Olympus
And at the point
      Where their bellies
Fill with laughter
      I
Fill their throats
      With lightning
I want them to
Feel
A razor blade of
Betrayal

I want them to
Feel this hurt
    But such an ending
Cannot be
    The wicked, indeed,
Lives forever
    But my love
Is so much stronger
    So much older
    So much wiser
I do not
    Have time
To cast this lightning
    This thunder

Instead I keep it
    Within me
Turning sugar
    Into salt
In my heart
    Will do nothing
So I do nothing
    But I remember
And I will not
    Laugh with them
Though I still feel
    Pain in my body
It is karma
    That keeps the score

OLD MAN BLOOD

The building still smells of blood
Heavy out the womb, hard on the floor
Someone else's DNA sticks under my shoes
He drinks again and again and slams beer down
Outside, sitting, in the heat, the cold, the rain
Says hi to me any chance he gets
Talks about car carburetors he used to work on
And I walk with his blood beneath my feet
Marks of it flowing from one end to the other
Early in the morning, I feel it sting my nose
Stings of old wounds and fresh copper
How much blood lives within this place
Leaks at home, then leaks in the hall
Old blood, new pumping, flows on, in and out, off and in
Morning for me, stepping on his blood

PART THREE: RESURRECTION

BULTOS

Bultos—
> in between worlds
> bumps in the road
> finding forks to go down

no *mija*
don't go down there

So, ok
> where do i go
> spirits take me everywhere
> my spirit is sensitive
unsure, unnerving

Weaving
> in and out and around, all over
> i feel the bumps
> then turn away
my spirit spirals throughout
> > and i return home

PINS AND NEEDLES

I wonder what her last thoughts were
When the injection in her arm
Needle to skin
Broke regrets in her decision
Was she fulfilled with such a short life?

I imagine that she was laying down
I don't know who was beside her
Maybe she was alone
Did she go with tears or a smile on her face?
Where is she now.

How comforting to think she chose
When to go
An article, simply explaining in the headlines:
"32 year old woman chooses to die for her birthday"
Is that considered a gift?
The struggle with her mind
Was far too great
          So she went

I sit at 32 years old now
Remembering my own thoughts
On pins and needles
The doctors explained to me, they injected me
All of my fears were revealed laying down
That time I could do nothing for myself
Were the threats of my body deteriorating real?
Would my body stop doing what it's told?

All my fears revealed, laying down
Struggling with confusion of what life
Was supposed to be
I could do nothing for myself
Fearful of my brain giving up

I must have felt just like her:
    Sometimes ready to die
    But not finding it within me to go
    When my final time with pins and needles comes
    I crave that I won't be alone

SCATTERED THOUGHTS

| girl | scary | > | hear my tone |
| tall | bitch | > | in every pitch |

HOW TO MAKE THE OLDEST DAUGHTER SPIN

A good daughter
A head that's strong

but i am tired
        world—where do i belong?

KILLING TRAUMA

When you begin
To unwrap the bandages
On your head
That have pressed assumptions
And thoughts
So deeply into your biology
Farther than the skin
On a micro level
It's hard to think
On a pinker scale
One intoxicated
With gentleness
That the ancestors gave you
One that you were born with
But found it hard to find
Everyone became a trail
Straying you further
And further
From your predesignated path
But now we are in a time
That such a soft pink
Held underneath
A delicate and tattered veil
Gets to emerge
As the tightening loosens

And we begin
To allow ourselves into
That kind of softness
And we are given that instruction
To lay into the signifying color
So that we find serenity
Empathy and divinity
In our lives and in our rest
The bandages on
Our eyes and wrists
Can come off now
Wipe that knowledge of the universe
And the fierce gentleness of the sea
Back into our being
The headache is gone now
It's time to be

FORCE IN THE CIRCUMSTANCE OF THE DEATHBED

Death is ambiguous, and we all must face it
Can we suffer any more in the meantime?
Old buildings filled with old screams tells us that we can
Compassion and self sacrifice are always overlooked
In this life, in all lives, a tick in the brain makes
That uncertainty so much more unbearable and
Ending the pain feels more comforting than anything else
We die in threes, the holy number
Wicked passions surround potential escape
Out of the deep holes of the mind
Diving deep, we question death—what it could be like
The feeling of death, I imagine, is a pool of warm golden water
Showered with petals and old memories of the past
Perhaps, even, a glimpse into other worlds and our lives next
How may we compassionately walk ourselves to the road of the end
The road, smooth and amongst the trees, beckons with glee
A type of glee that at once may have been ambivalent
Ambiguous with its intentions, now welcoming
We do suffer now and may again suffer
The same wrongdoings and ill intentions of the past
But as we dive into the gold water after walking the cold road
These will be some type of beauty
That has made it all worth it

MOON AND CROW

It is very hard to walk in between multiple dimensions
I am always learning about myself, embracing rage and fear
 One who speaks directly with the ocean
 One who speaks directly to the mountain
 One who speaks directly into the fire
I watch the moon and the crow kiss one another
Signaling that darkness always kisses the light
 Men flirting with stars
 Always get burned
They cannot hold such beauty in their hands
Possessing a slippery reward they will never understand
 Those who speak directly to the dead
 Those who speak directly to their pain
 Those who speak directly into strangled laughter
Once upon a time I could not be with myself
Because I was much too scared, and did not want to
Sick with motives when moving around the decades
Happy to be deep with the world in the ways of the ancestors
Speaking directly to them, kindness and knowledge in their eyes
So
I swear to pursue and pay attention when winds call to me
Walk on the street, gasp in memory, deliver imagination
Thriving in the fields of flowers that continue to love me
Love places that never change and remind me to never stay the same
Some faces that bring me comfort and I love so much
A lot of pressure in my heart that pumps in me, alive
Alive and still walking in beauty and inbetween multiple dimensions

FUNERAL POEMS

Another round of a funeral poem
Although, it is for someone I do not know
Already, other people hold my words in their hands
Another round of goodbyes, burning as the world turns
    I am tired

Tired of being the spot writer that everybody knows
Funeral poem writer, eulogy digger in residence
Didn't think this was a world I'd be a part of
Always finding words, bringing them to the dead, the both burn

Will my body be covered in words also?
My time is coming up, at some point, I hope not too soon
But I hope that I am buried
In a mixture fragrance of flowers and ink

For now I have to write something
Have to write it down while the walls cry black
Death comes soon, and how easily we want to forget
What is coming up in the near future will always die

Someone, something, a city, a comfort, a place
How to replace things when you couldn't afford the first
In the first place
And how they are rewarded when everything is lost: alone,
    cold, confused

Water not even available, fire in lieu of sanctuary
Death comes soon, ashes mixed with blood
Animals gone, water poisoned
    Who will answer for this
    Who will answer for their death

DEATH ABC'S

Another round of a funeral poem
Although for someone I do not know
Already, other people hold my words in their hands
Another round of goodbyes

Burning as the world turns
Bodies that were once people, pumped with fluid or turned to ash
Beautiful, I see them, and my aunt takes pictures of her
Brother in a casket, a job that I hope I'll never have

Can be written as dry as a bone, these pages
Comforting also to not have to say these words out loud in soggy places
Communicate your love directly to them, gone
Considered as unbecoming from this planet, spilling phrases no one
       wants to hear

Death is an interesting prompt that no writer is prepared for
Death comes too soon, ashes mixed with blood, words blurred by emotion
Death is imminent, and ye I cannot get too comfortable
Dying shyly walks in and my words with them walk out

STILL

Most people die at 15 but we wait until 65 to bury them. As a kid, I witnessed the funeral of my baby cousin and remember the frantic electricity of my parents when we pulled up to the hospital to see what was going on. I don't remember getting out of the car.

But the body was a sheepish blue: pale little face, closed baby doll eyelids and I knew what was going on but didn't understand. Mom worked in medicine so never hid anything from us; but it became abundantly clear this was a serious matter when the adults told all the cousins to stop giggling from behind the pews.

I walked up to see her but I was afraid and intrigued by death—how can something be shut so quickly, end so indefinitely, if we were also little but kept on living? What was it about us where we stood out of the casket, the element we had that she didn't?

Her last home was so tiny, and she looked even tinier in it. The church felt cold and quiet and I imagined what she must have felt like, if she could feel anymore; I didn't know what it meant to not be able to feel then, but I would find out much later in life.

I remember it being warm when I think about her small grave; there were many tears and mention of angel wings, balloons in the air and hugs that I had to give. This felt like a pain that was not mine to witness, but we were family, and that's how it is.

When I lost my own son I began to hear stories of other women who lost others also. Women I had known all my life who bore more stress, legendary medical issues and souls to be returned to Heaven than children, but who never forgot the pain in that loss.

It is easy to want to die because then every other type of pain
we experience is forgotten so easily; there is a sentiment of "rest
in peace" that we don't get in life, and thus the vicious cycle of
wanting to die once again makes sense. I have tried at least 7 times.

But when you are forced to die, then you topple over the pieces
in your life that put you together, eyes widen and mouths shrink;
voices wither and skin changes. The smell of life altered and death
rolls altogether. Quickly, when you die, others feel themselves die
with you.

So at 65 I wonder how many times I will have died over and over;
maybe this is something to revisit when I get to this age. Perhaps
now it feels a bit morbid, but there is a joy in being able to write
about a universal experience, for all ages, and in the millions of
ways that people understand.

I think about all the other people that have to be buried into
the ground or stored in boxes and urns that lie around the house.
In the ways that I continue to speak to people I love when other
people try to tell me these people are gone; between baby to
broken down, there are layers of time where we have lived.

I've never had to push the button that makes one transform from
body to ash, but I think of three people I know who have. It is
a type of bravery that I think we need more of, because then we
really get to ask IF we want to die and have the honor of sending
them into another type of life.

Dreams can be effective with death, and don't always take place immediately; instead, I am still beside the campfire with my uncle who died from stomach cancer and threw up black bile, apologetically, as I began to think of the words that would form in the letter I wrote for him that his longtime partner would eventually read when they were alone, and would end up in his hands when they placed him in the cold granite vault alongside the other veterans.

I am still singing the original version of *The Phantom of the Opera* with my musical grandmother, who in the time I knew her, was bound by her wheelchair but managed to get around and would leave constant voicemails reminding us of her love and buying us candy when she herself could not afford to eat. In my thoughts and dreams, I am still a little girl abused by her sons who finds solace in her lap as she reads me poetry and reminds me to hide behind corridors of light when Shadow People want to run after me.

I am still near the river with one of my Great Grandmothers whom I never knew in life but have always known in death, because my mother and grandmother refused to let her die and eventually gave me a place in these women to call home and take care of. She is the person whose last name took. Change mine to because we are both healers. Allows me to forgive myself on the mountain when I felt like my own greatest failure.

I am still in a room filled with lots of people I don't know because I am here for a girl who bears my first name, who died in a way that I almost did, and that drains my mind when I am at the funeral because I am still on heavy medication and feel my emotions slip away, to imagine what this would have been like if she had been me. I dream of the cries and screams of my brother and my friends, and the difficulty they have in going up to see her because they could not carry the thought of remembering that now, that is how she is.

I am still in the house of my other Great Grandmother. The house had a mask by the front door that would often scare me. Dark hallways filled with ghosts, including the baby that she had lost. Her backyard will always feel like a sanctuary and warm, unlike the church where her service was held in. In the pews I held my breath until I heard the choir sing and started weeping. My little eyes watched one of my uncles in the only time I've ever seen him weeping, and the other stand from a distance under a tree at her burial because the loss of his mother was just too much for him; he always joked that he was her favorite and she'd wave him away, but never fully said "no."

I am still in Mexico with a new family that was a big part of my mother's childhood, surrounded by people who aren't wailing because many of us were there when she no longer was. The grave is glittered with floral arrangements of all shapes, colors and sizes, that once stood near her casket in the church that people slept by on inflatable mattresses and on hard pews; such is the testament to Mexican love. The shapes of people moving in the church and in the graveyard; the colors of flowers fading in the sunshine; the size of Rosarito walking to the curbs to say goodbye as we drive by. I am still holding her hand in the living room, witnessing the last parts of her spirit leave this Earth, just like everybody else.

Somehow, I am still.

B

I met my son for the first time
When I was 30 years old
He came to me with an inquisitive mind
A brave little warrior
Fierce in his blood
And in his heart

He came in the form
Of my uncles' sperm
My rapists' seed
Behind my parents' bedroom
And in front of glass doors

But he taught me to play
With hands so gentle
Small, but mighty
"I'll come back someday"
He tells me again

I know it, and I believe him
The drums tell it to me too
My ancestors strike down trees
With machetes, to make my way
To and for him

I don't want to say that he is lost
Because in many ways
He still finds me
Affectionately, caressing
The spininess that has been programmed
In my heart

SAME FACE, OTHER ANGLE

for the first time i see her face
    from a different angle
i take it all in, this familiar face
    from another perspective
my tea kettle calls
    bubbling with deep red liquid
the rose petals float
    little manta rays rising to the surface
until they sink down, down into the deep
    little manta rays below the waves
then a great sudden sadness
    pushes me away, stirring in my tea
    arrives, suspicious upon entry
i name my goodbyes to
    lily pads and sleepless nights
impressed that i'm alive
    dark lipstick
        silky apparitions
            velvet that you'll miss
i make this night all about me
                because
for the first time i see my face
from a different angle
take her all in, her familiar face
from another perspective

ITS OWN PIECE

I have no regrets
I have no desire to hold on
To what the past
Made me
I remember
Like in those moments
I remember what I do

What I have to

I give up
On the notion that these are
All the pieces
That make me
That I can fly higher
Heading towards the sun

But unlike Icarus I
Stand and shall not fall
Like the birds I will find my wind
And dance for what is to come
Before the blazing star
Burns and leaves my mind

I know that I had to

Reaching for some unfamiliar face
Some unfamiliar figure
I
Tried to do all that I can and
I
Am lucky to still even be here

I have no regrets
For many who see the sun
There is a burning nightmare
But I
Do not fear it
I have been accustomed to its
Thrusting its rays on me
And so I bounce them back

I am sorry to the dear boy
Who even with wings
Fell so far down
But I will not
   I cannot
Do the same
Even if the past
Comes back to visit me

Every now and again
It haunts me like a cat
On the windowsill but I
Look back at it with sun
Filled eyes
And I
Make sure it does not look away

I am beyond everything
That I had to do
Hotels—alleys—clubs—classes
Beyond all of this
And into the next
The past holds
No future for me here

PEPPER

Sometimes I dream of you so much I forget that you're not here
Sometimes I think of your eyes and all the kindness within them
    that I will never see again

When a tornado is coming, people generally say that if you look
    right at it and it doesn't move, its coming for you
But what of the spirits that I see in old spaces and familiar hallways,
    that also do not move
Do I walk or let them stand still?

I'm sad that I barely remember the sound of your voice but
Sometimes I dream of being in your house again, outside and
    in, not knowing any of the toxic family drama
Sometimes I wish you'd seen so much of what I have done
    and all that I've become as a living being on earth

Things are so different now—I don't know how to escape it
When the fires blew out, I thought about home and I thought about
    you and I thought about how much that house meant to me
Renovating the house, the electricians wondered how yours hadn't
    gone up in flames way before

I am drowning in life and I feel that only you can save me
Desperately, I tried to track down the old footage of you so that
I could again hear your voice
Erased, they said, old traces of that *correo electronico* gone into
the ether and far, far away
I've cried at the loss of you before but this felt like
A final blow I was not prepared for and again
When the fires broke out, I broke out into tears at the thought
of your house being gone

What happens when a cemetery is on fire
When the dead bleed again and soak the soil with formaldehyde
Do they go up aflame again just as easily as us, who are living
I hope you never burn
I hope the only way that you burn is through my heart, and in
the worlds that form a lump in my throat that I wish I could
say but right now: I cannot speak them

Sometimes I want to go back into your arms, before the diagnoses,
before I knew your awareness of pain, before my parents were gone
Sometimes I think of your eyes and how much I looked at you before
they closed the casket and wish you'd open them again

I know I hold a lot of wishes
But I wish to continue your kindness the most

EUTHANASIA, DIAGNOSIS III

How can I describe how many times I have died with you
My body—
Struck by the lightning of your jealousy and insecurity
grows limp and deconstructs
like a doll
you stuff me with pieces of anger and doubt
and i don't know how to get it out

so i take scissors to myself

i cut them out and
arrange them lie dead flowers from an
arrangement given to me by
Your Mother

i   splay   them   out
and try to redirect myself like this

(to strike any instance of ever going back):

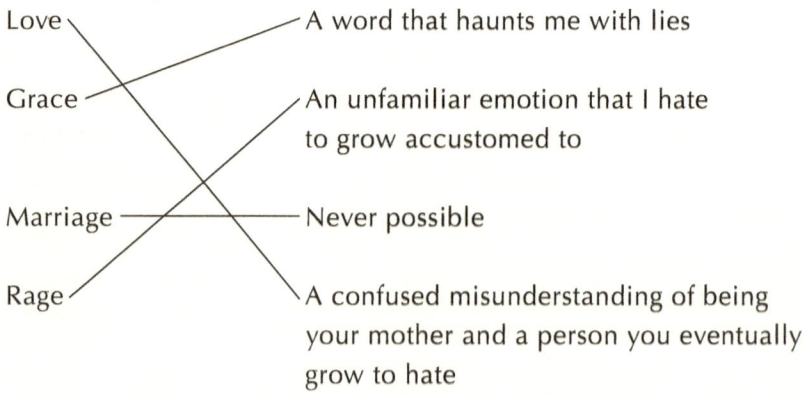

Love — A word that haunts me with lies

Grace — An unfamiliar emotion that I hate
to grow accustomed to

Marriage — Never possible

Rage — A confused misunderstanding of being
your mother and a person you eventually
grow to hate

I've had to kill myself so many times for you.
And my bloodied heart still is not enough; words of sugar turn into
poison, affection rots under the grounds of trauma with deceit, and
you become a surgeon crafting my body in ways I didn't want to
know were possible. Removing my eyes so I could never see myself
the same, extracting my tongue so I could never speak to you how
I needed to, disintegrated my brain and integrity to bend under the
smoothness of your knife. Removing every part of me became
surgical—and you were swift.

But my death time and time again gave me permission to snap
around the darkest corridors of my mind and behind it I began the
excavation of softness of who I was before you, the manifestation
process began after you removed these parts of me, but I have found
them again.

I am growing myself back and your knife has rusted.

"UGLY"

I once had a partner who told me I wasn't beautiful enough.
Who told me after seeing a photo of me from years ago and
said that my exes were lucky because I was "in my prime"
back then. Who once got so drunk that they ended up at the
beach on one knee, asking for my hand, not long after putting
theirs on me. To this day, my jaw hurts whenever I talk.

When I think of the way
I've brushed up with death
There are some times I wonder
How I felt worse with you

I think of what is beautiful to you
Before my body hits the floor
Cold tile meets my shrieking limbs that seize
Symptoms of your perverted definition

"Why can't you show more grace?"
Grace: An acceptance of my fall,
An acceptance of your tragedy
Absorbing that no matter what, I'd always be ugly

In my prime meant in my head
Meant understanding my abuse
Starving myself for your desired body
Priming myself as a dying doll

As I laid down, facing fate
Under fluorescent lights
In the hospital
It was much easier than you

The breathing beneath
My broken body was less
Suffocating then
The loneliness you made me choke on

I hope now that I am dead to you
Truly, in your mind
Bury me beneath your emotions
Do not mourn me

FOR J., A CEMETERY ODE

It starts in the golden hour
When I walk between the cyprus
And between the streets of the cemetery

Today, the graves are flowered
With orange oceans
An aftermath from the day of the dead

I wonder and wander as I look around
Take in the names and dates
Faces beneath the ground
When the decorations are taken away, where do they go?

There is a connection of manners
Between all the strangers here
I sit on the benches and witness life before me

Young men yelling about themselves
Turn quiet when they remember
Why they are there

There are four at first
The volume changes when they remember
Some have to leave; the color orange becomes pain

I briefly visit the grave of a girl
That I hardly got to know
She was the friend of some of my friends

There was no orange at her plot
But I wipe away thick grime of dust
And there, I can see her face

My notebook is on the grass, above where she lay
But I could not find words for the page
And I listen, the wind comes, and I pray

The boys are still yelling
And in the distance I see
More of the dead across the street

I wait for a few cars to pass
And then I am with them
And then I read more about when they were alive

I turn on the cornered path
Then I hear *corridos* of death behind me
From a *señor* sitting by an ornate, orange space

His truck marks the dates of his loss
Many thoughts pass but I wonder as I wander
Does he have a cemetery playlist?

Death and life blend into the same song

Amor eterno—something that connects us all
The boys are there for their friend
Señor there for another boy lost
And I am there
For a girl that I hardly got to know

LOSE

One day you will kill me
One day I will die
One day my blood will run cold

      One day you will know
           One day you will know
                One day you will know

I am losing
Untold

                    Am I losing myself?

STAY WITH ME

I am here at a funeral for a mother of a mother
Old Catholic rituals come alive in me again
On my knees, praying like a lady
I've missed my pearls this time
But I pay respects
As best I can
I've never seen you cry so much before
And like my mother, these tears pierce me
I feel like a daughter in these times
Others' mothers ask me not to leave
Hold on to me
You tell me
Stay with me
And I respond
That I will never go

EVERYTHING WE DO, IS BECAUSE WE DIE

1.
Choosing to die is not the same as genocide
I live in the body of someone
Who comes from a body
That remembers open bodies
And blood
On the floors of her country
And no legal act of
Dignified Death
Voluntary Death
orTermination of Life
Would have changed that
Is it not a homicide
When you can't choose when you can't remember
When the hands who held your children are gone
When the chains infringing your mind can't be broken
Why do we the living care about the choice of the soon to be dead
What if they want to remember
How they'll be remembered
Like my ancestors who took out loved ones from the house
    Feet first
Or how like now I remember the dead more than once a year
    More like once a day
Where is the law involved when telling my people how to grieve?

What
Is the point
Of obsessing
Over the prolongation
Of life expectancy
When some people
Do not want to live it

2.

The future cannot last if our people are not well
They argue:
    "It is cruel and selfish
    To choose to die
    Against God, Against Law
    Against God's Law"

But where were they when I held a blade in my hand
Or when my mother—saw her family slaughtered
Heard that my uncle died
At the end of a machete to his head
Paid for by their
Charitable dollars
Tax write offs
And sympathy
Soaked deep in blood

How can they claim
To be pro life
When not too far from here their blood money
Funds the genocide that was to build a better future
Why don't they speak up
For people who did not choose to die

It was said in an article not too long ago that many people found it offensive when a Dutch doctor watched his patient die in a euthanasia pod. She died beneath the trees, at her request; isn't it funny how the feelings of these requests change when we choose them before our bodies grow cold. Plans for the dead are made, families and friends march towards the body and the grief begins again and again. But to be in a place between dead and choosing not to be alive is a strange, contradictory "controversy" to me. Euthanasia, in its original Greek form, means "eu" (good) and "thánatos" (death). Genocide, in its original Greek form, means "genos" (race) mixed with the Latin ending "cide" (killing). What is good for the former turns sour by the latter, with the level of violence being the difference in choice.

How we have strayed away from its meaning and butchered its belief to make it our own. Choosing to die is not the same as choosing to watch genocide.

CAN'T HELP THAT YOU'RE WANTING TO DIE

I hear how much you want to die
Somewhere that I've been before
The wanting to die and the wanting to save
My hands reach out to
Something lesser than air
Something lesser than nothing
It's a gory realization that I
Have no space for you, in life and death
There is nothing left in this goodbye
I simply walk away
You beg but I do not listen
And can't help that you're wanting to die
That you weep because you have lost your mind
There is nothing I can do to help you find it
I swear at a god you wish for me to worship
Think about all the curses that I am breaking
How I am saving my ancestors past and children future
How I am saving myself now
From not being a part of you
I'm sorry that you want to die
    I'm sorry that you want to die
But I want to live so much more

HOW TO KEEP THE BLOOD INSIDE

It's taken me so, so long
To learn how to keep the blood inside
Every now and again it is tempting
To open my skin and let some out
But I don't want that rush anymore
Have to remember the
Delicate nature of my wrists
Soothe the old flames that make me hurt
Cool the pain that once overtook me
I remember myself, remember my blood
That belongs inside, belongs to me
Turn to my words to flirt with my agony
Leave my ache in ink rather than blood
Say goodbye to the mystique of suicide
That my stars and my blood
Recall my time that I've spent on here
Don't take it for granted again
My heart yearns for things other than sorrow
My blood rushes again to the head
I awake from the darkness
And know that I will always get better

HOW DO WE SIT IN THE DARKNESS?

Listening to the calls and trying to avoid resistance
I don't need to do, I just need to be
    All unfolds
Walking through life as an expansive being
Acknowledging those who cannot receive you
Perpetuating systems of violence to fit in
Tapping into the primal self
Avoiding self-harm
Even when we don't feel connected, we are
Experiencing beautiful deaths lead to power
Synchronicity in space and time together
Embracing authentic lessons in fear
Use medicine, don't drift off, power of presence
Dance grief ritual, methods of letting go
Listening when the body is loud—don't abuse the body
Not overdoing, going slower, loving the self
Die many times, death, fear, repeat, dying
Grief in the lungs—breathing—self control
Paying attention to unintentional isolation
Do this every day, and give darkness
Time worthwhile

HEART LESSONS

I've been paying attention to everybody
Else's heart, that I've forgot about mine
When was the last time I let my heart play?
Sometimes poetics are just poetics and there is,
For all intents and purposes, no rhyme or reason
    In that
Maybe love can be the same, when in the moment
It's all tension and passion, then as you get to be
All too familiar, and you start to see the flaws
Even in the things you deem to be the most perfect

It's good to pay attention to the vessel, its chambers
Science tells us what the chambers do, and
What they are meant for,
But if I'd look in those four chambers,
What do I find?
Are there distinctive lines
Between my veins of actual happiness or hints of
Jealousy? Do I expose myself too vulnerable,
Even though I laugh through the desire of
Having someone be prepared to know my
Heart still bleeds

Is there such a thing as caring for the heart too
Much? Would that lead to the heart in your brain
Versus the heart of your heart, in the chest, do
They know each other?
Brain heart causes the heart to become self-conscious
And aware
What is the science behind when
The heart gets too shy?

BREAKING UP WITH SUICIDE

I don't want to do this the easy way
Instead, I want to feel everything
Death by a million cuts
Prolong my relationship from you as long as possible
So, we'll have to break up
You'll come back around
Begging me to come back
Promise something better with pretty smiles
With loaded weapons behind your back
But I am so much better now
The temptation of you will not work on me
Sure, there will be times that I will want to
Want to give you what you want
Give all of myself to you
But you are banned from my wrist
Banished from my neck
Repelled from going inside me
I'm not doing this the easy way
Because this is not just for me
But for me and everyone after me
I will take all the lessons you've given me
And move on
I can't keep breaking
So I'm breaking up
With you

PRETTY HAIR

I want my hair to be curly
But I don't wanna be pretty
See, because
Being pretty to me means
Being molested
Your inches reflect
The numbers of my age
When you entered me
And also when you
Pulled out
I don't like it when
People have to touch my hair because
These are the people I trust
And when they touch my hair
I
Remember
You
And then I don't
Trust them anymore

And I know
That
This is all your fault because I
Was a literal child
I
Didn't understand what was going on
Any four year old couldn't
And then at eight you told me
That I was too old
But didn't we have fun
And I nodded because
I didn't know what you meant
When you held out your hand
Unfurled them between my curls and
Told me how pretty I was

It's taken me a long time to remember
How to safely be a girl
I can be pretty all on my own
Even curl my own hair
And know that within these rituals
I hold a power
Because I don't always remember you
And I am not confused about what happened
Like grandpa once told me
I do know
But it is in this knowing that I understand

What I couldn't have done
How much patience I am owed
Understanding love like no other
Understanding letting go
Understanding the evil of your benevolence
And where I need to go
And it is far away from you
Every year I grow farther from your
Version of being pretty
And evolve into my own
Instead

I'LL BE YOUR HUCKLEBERRY

Every time the scene where Val Kilmer's character dies, you laugh
I didn't understand then, but I know why now
There is something inherently funny about death
A man dies on the screen and the happiness echoes through your belly
We would later laugh around your death bed
Where you would laugh with us one last time
Until the tubes entered your body
Until you tried to take them off
And my mother telling you to keep it on
Until it wasn't what you wanted
Until she told you it was fine if you wanted to go
The same eyes that looked at me
Closed tighter
Harder now
I wouldn't catch you laughing when the rain came down
Wouldn't sing with you anymore when my uncles made jokes
        while you were dying
Wouldn't hear you reading to me to soothe the wounds of your sons
I didn't laugh when I realized that you would really die

The TV screens would play
Idontknowwhat
Because I was too focused on you
Crying for you when that same rain came down
Lost god in the chapel when they told us you would not be coming back
It would take me a long while to be able to laugh again
But I don't regret being there to hold your hand
To softly repeat the words we shared from one apartment to the next
Words we heard as you chased comfort from one run-down facility
        to the next
We shared one final performance about bubblegum on a bedpost
The last time I would hear you laugh
I still miss you but time has passed
And when I see this same scene, now I can laugh
Repeating some of your favorite words
Laughing as the cowboy dies
Remembering how much you wrapped me in your love
Death, tore us apart, but I remember
That I'll always be your huckleberry

INSANITY & WIND

I had another round of insanity recently
        But as always, I feel better
I'm feeling myself in another dimension again
        It's very Victorian in here
My arms are so sore
        But my body functions
So for that, I suppose I can be grateful
        The wind if telling a lot lately
But I am far away enough
        From it that I can actually appreciate it
But for everyone in my hometown
        I mourn
Some days I research old asylums
        Because these places feel familiar to me
I write and read more and more
        Wild dreams last through the night
And I saw someone who I came to love
        That shared their love with someone else
With women that I could never be
        Women ever so happy, women never in asylums
So instead I will drift between insanity and the wind
        Hoping I don't stand in my own way

HELP + MEDICINE

Field of grass
Seeking across the green
I see myself again
A new dimension
Better self
To help someone else

Looking inside
On their inside
Tiny levels of pain
Uncertainty and suffering
Turned into brevity and gold
I help them return home

DELAYED DEATH SCENARIO

My life has been a long, delayed earth scenario
Razors graze my skin now, but not to dig deep
Cliff Sides are only meant for looking over
Needles pierce my skin only when the doctor needs them

Sometimes when I sit, death sits beside me
As I lay down, it rounds the corner and reminds me
How swiftly I could die, how close I've been to it before
So many times—and then I remember how it's taken others

Delaying itself, in my face every time I think it's gone
Witnessing blood in bags, hospital beds, turning gurneys
Coffins become cousins, with spaces unrelated
Because it is not in these boxes where I rest yet

Instead I walk above mossy plots and gated grounds
Time slows down and I spend more of it learning how to live
Old stings don't hurt so severely and my mind
   Grows old, gets delayed

But I no longer allow myself to always welcome death in
So that I am right here, in my right mind
Death: I do see you
You'll just have to delay from me

                              one more time

TWO BIRDS

I watched two birds fly through the sky today
Over the sunset, they played with each other
How good it must feel to love
With wind beneath these wings
I turned around quickly
To watch the beauty behind me
I felt I was missing
And it grew ablaze
Glorious abundance
In distinct colors split between the clouds
Down the middle
Above, stained hues of red marries with light gold
Poked through underneath
I keep staring
As if I could ever look long enough where
My brain could comprehend what lay before me
Or as if this would be the last thing that I
Would remember
In my last moments alive
It's attached deep into my memory
And then the birds fly back
Their graceful waves keep me here
Dare me not to look away
Watch the clouds and feel the sun
Delicate lines of beauty and fear grow within
     And then
     I am free
Myself again, grounded for now, lone bird
Flying in her own sky
Learning how to use these wings again

Resources

It is a lifelong process to learn how to take care of yourself, and when to seek support when you've felt like you've had enough. Below is a small list of resources, but please also reach out to your communities, write, dance, read, cry if you need to. Though I am a firm believer that anyone should have the right and the resources to leave this Earth in their own way, I also believe that it is worth the effort to feel supported until the end.

ORGANIZATIONS
988 Lifeline
International Association for Suicidal Prevention
National Institute of Mental Health
Suicide Prevention Alliance

Books
Perfect, by Natasha Friend
Braiding Sweetgrass, by Robin Wall Kimmerer
Borderlands/La Frontera, by Gloria Anzaldua
The Tibetan Book of Living and Dying by Sogyal Rinpoche
A Graceful Exit by Lofty L. Basta
Euthanasia and Assisted Suicide by Michael J. Cholbi
Hindu Ethics: Purity, Abortion, and Euthanasia
      by Harold G. Coward, Julius J. Lipner, Katherine K. Young
Facing Death: Where Culture, Religion, and Medicine Meet
      by Howard M. Spiro, Mary G. McCrea Curnen,
      and Lee Palmer Wandel
From Here to Eternity: Traveling the World to Find the
      Good Death by Caitlin Doughty
Loud in the House of Myself: Memoir of a Strange Girl, by Stacy Pershall

Instagram Accounts to Follow

@nalgonapositivitypride

@florycantoacademy

@littlesunnydoodles

@yesikastarr

@Thehoodwitch

@dont_gaslight_me_bruh

@abejarise

@spiritrootmedicinepeople

@crushingcolonialism

@sooshinalisisterproject

@thedeathnetwork

@okuntakinte

ABOUT THE AUTHOR

Jessica (she/her/*ella*) is a Two Spirit, Latina *y Xicana* femme from the San Fernando Valley, who is a published poet, community organizer, and educator. When she is not working, she is taking long walks and exploring nature, learning new recipes, or reading lots of books. Aside from this collection of poems, she will have a chapter focusing on life as a queer *Salvadoreña* published next year in the *Engendering U.S. Central American Women & Womxn's Testimonio* through the University of Arizona Press.

When she is not writing, she is also organizing and attending Two Spirit powwows and ceremonies and serving as one of the co-chairs for the Bay Area American Indian Two Spirits (BAAITS) powwow, and multiple theater projects. She enjoys spending time with friends and family, and learning German and Nahuatl.

She can be found on Instagram through her personal account: @tzapotl_flores and her literary account where she shares book reviews and author insight on all her writing projects: @tzapotl.lit

She holds a Dual M.A. from Claremont Graduate University in English and Cultural Studies and Dual B.A. from the University of California Riverside in English and *Chicane* Studies.

She wishes many blessings to you, and hopes that these words resonate with you. *Tlazocamati, Ometeotl, Gracias,* Thank You.

Publisher's Note

Daxson publishing was created to help marginalized artists publish their work, so the world can hear their voice. The vision for this publishing house is to help people get their work out there, and not have them struggle finding their way through the publishing process. Everyone's voice deserves to be heard, and we are here to help. If you are interested in submitting a manuscript, email daxsonpublishing@gmail.com. Support our cause! Buy our books at daxsonpublishing.com.